INFOMOJIS

SPACE

WAYLAND
www.waylandbooks.co.uk

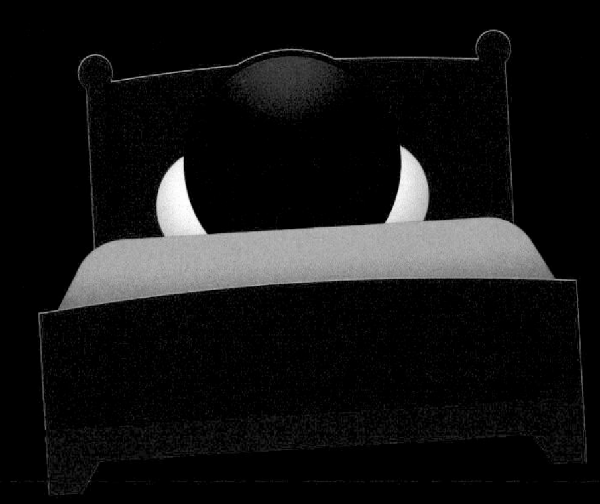

First published in Great Britain
in 2018 by Wayland

Editor: Amy Pimperton
Produced by Tall Tree Ltd
Editor: Jon Richards
Designer: Ed Simkins

ISBN: 978 1 5263 0672 2

Wayland
An imprint of Hachette Children's Group
Part of Hodder and Stoughton
Carmelite House
50 Victoria Embankment
London EC4Y 0DZ

An Hachette UK Company
www.hachette.co.uk
www.hachettechildrens.co.uk

Printed and bound in China

This book uses different units to measure different things:

Distance is measured in kilometres (km), astronomical units (AU – the distance between the Sun and Earth) and light years (the distance light travels in a year).

Area is measured using square kilometres (sq km).

Mass is measured using kilograms (kg) and megatons.

Temperature is measured in degrees Celsius (°C) and Kelvin (K).

Speed is measured using kilometres per hour (kph).

THE SOLAR SYSTEM

Earth may be a big place, but it's just one of eight planets that spin around the burning ball of gas that is our Sun. Together, they are known as the Solar System.

Great balls of fire
The Sun is the biggest object in the Solar System, and sits in the middle of the Solar System. Powerful forces deep inside the Sun produce huge amounts of energy. This energy is thrown out into space and it warms the planets and other objects that spin around it.

The planets
The eight worlds that orbit the Sun are all very different.

The four inner planets are Mercury, Venus, Earth and Mars. They are known as rocky planets, because they are made largely from rock.

Mars

Earth

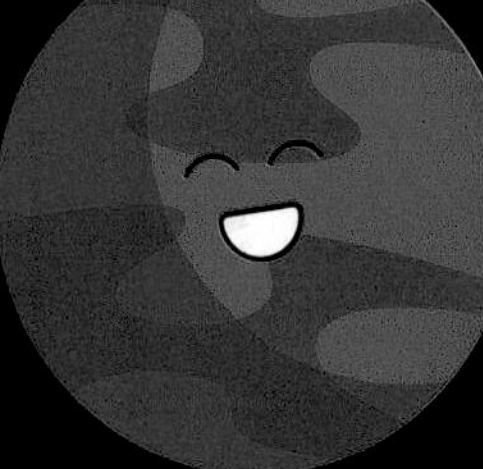

Venus

Mercury

The French mathematician Urbain Le Verrier (1811–1877) didn't need a telescope to find the planet Neptune. Instead, in 1845, he used good old mathematics to predict where the planet would be. The following year, astronomers in Berlin, Germany, found the planet exactly where Le Verrier said it would be!

Sun at the centre

Before the 16th century, many people believed that Earth was at the centre of the Solar System. Until Nicolaus Copernicus (1473–1543) came along, that is. The Polish astronomer made detailed studies of the planets and put forward the idea that the Sun was at the centre of the Solar System and Earth orbited around it.

NICOLAUS COPERNICUS

The four outer planets are Jupiter, Saturn, Uranus and Neptune. Jupiter and Saturn are known as gas giants because they are largely made from gas. Uranus and Neptune are known as ice giants, because … you guessed it … they're made largely from ice!

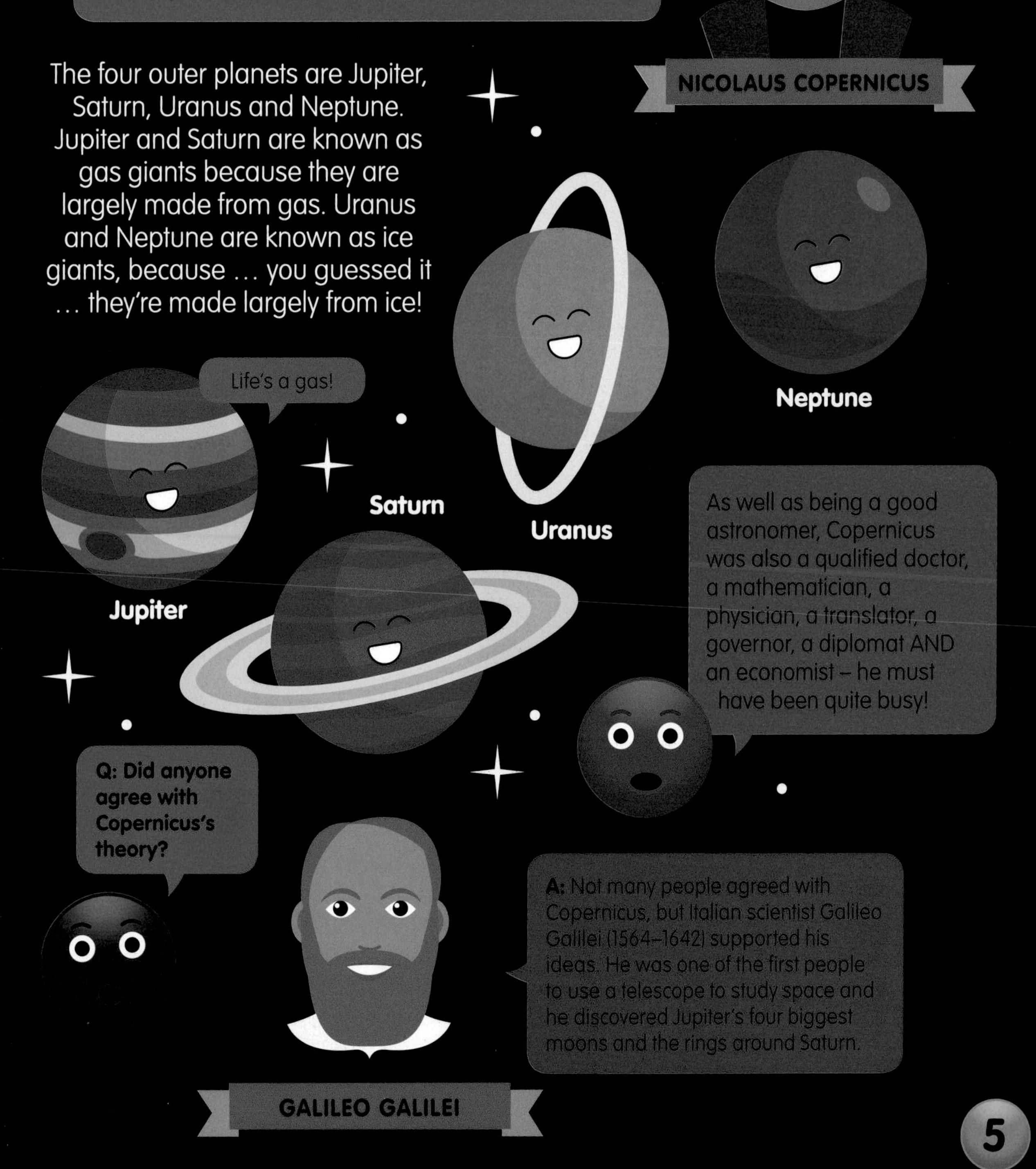

As well as being a good astronomer, Copernicus was also a qualified doctor, a mathematician, a physician, a translator, a governor, a diplomat AND an economist – he must have been quite busy!

Q: Did anyone agree with Copernicus's theory?

A: Not many people agreed with Copernicus, but Italian scientist Galileo Galilei (1564–1642) supported his ideas. He was one of the first people to use a telescope to study space and he discovered Jupiter's four biggest moons and the rings around Saturn.

GALILEO GALILEI

THE SUN

Even though it's 150 million km away, the Sun still feels hot on a summer's day. But get close up to this burning ball of gas and things really start to heat up!

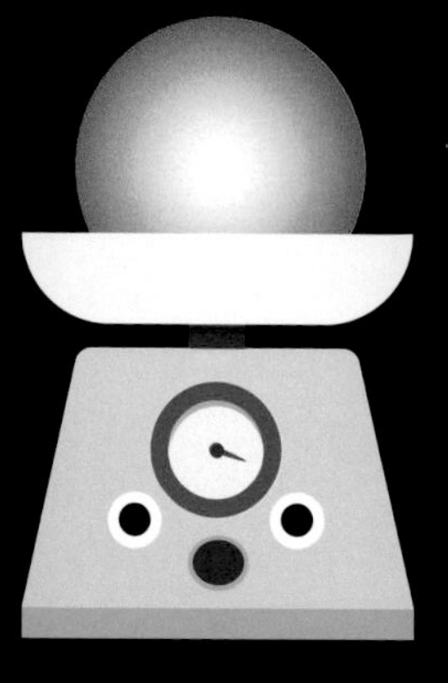

Giant of the Solar System
The Sun makes up about 99.8% of the Solar System's mass.

core

Nuclear fusion
Deep inside the core of the Sun, the force of gravity is so strong that atomic nuclei are fused together. This releases energy, which makes its way to the Sun's surface and is released into space.

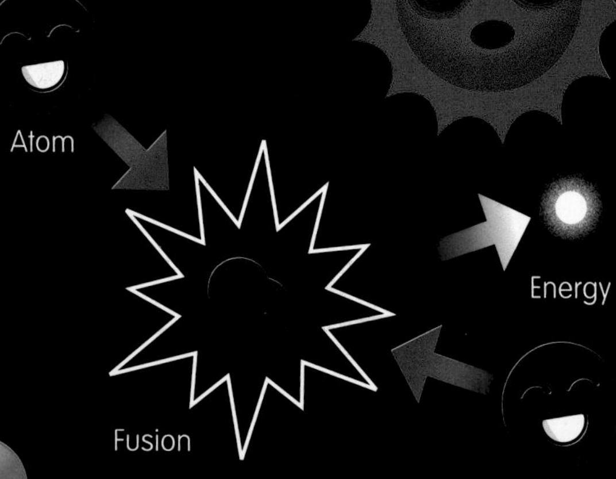

Q: How long does light take to travel from the Sun to Earth?

A: 8 minutes and 20 seconds!

This energy travels through space and we can see some of it as light. This energy also heats up the surface of Earth, warming it and the atmosphere above it. As the atmosphere warms up it swirls about creating the winds and weather we experience.

radiative zone

convective zone

photosphere

Deep in the core the temperature soars to 15 million °C. Outside the core are the radiative zones and the convective zones, where the temperature drops to JUST 2 million °C. At the surface, or photosphere, the Sun's temperature is a scorching 5,500 °C.

Energy can take more than one million years to travel from the core to the surface as it is continually absorbed and emitted by the tightly packed atomic nuclei.

Every now and then, the Sun throws out powerful bursts of radiation called solar flares. These bursts can disrupt radio communications and GPS equipment.

The Sun is about 150 million km from Earth. Astronomers call this distance 1 astronomical unit (AU) and use it to describe distances across the Solar System.

EARTH AND MOON

Earth is a very special place. It's the only planet we know where life exists, and its place in the Solar System as well as its atmosphere, land and water, create a unique planet with a wide range of ecosystems.

Too cold!

Just right!
Earth orbits in a region of space called the Goldilocks zone. This is a distance from the Sun where conditions aren't too hot or too cold for liquid water to exist, but, just like Goldilocks's porridge in the children's story, they are just right.

Too hot!

Just right!

Earth facts
Circumference: 40,030.2 km
Distance from Sun: about 150 million km
Year: about 365 days
Axis tilt: 23.4 degrees from the vertical

The Moon

THE MOON

Earth has one natural satellite – the Moon. It was formed about 4.5 billion years ago, when Earth was still young. An enormous object slammed into Earth, throwing up huge amounts of debris. This debris joined together to form the Moon.

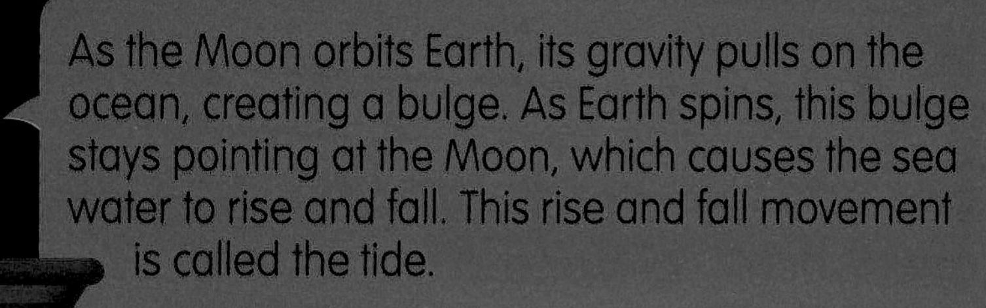

While many robot probes have visited, orbited, slammed into and landed on the Moon, only 12 people have ever set foot on its surface. These astronauts took part in the Apollo space programme, which successfully landed six missions on the Moon from 1969 to 1972.

Moon facts
Circumference: 10,917 km
Distance from Earth: 362,600–405,400 km
Time to orbit Earth: about 27 days
Axis tilt: 1.5 degrees

During the Apollo 17 mission in 1972, astronaut Eugene Cernan (1934–2017) set a Lunar land-speed record of 18 kph driving the Lunar Roving Vehicle.

The first robotic vehicles to explore the surface of another body in the Solar System were sent to the Moon. In 1970 and 1973, the Soviet Union sent two robot rovers called *Lunokhod 1* and *Lunokhod 2*, which zoomed around the Moon at a speedy 2 kph!

GETTING INTO SPACE

Space officially starts 100 km above Earth's surface. This may not seem like much, but getting that high requires really powerful rockets.

Rockets reach space using stages. When the engines in the first stage have used up their fuel, then the first stage separates and the engines in the next stage fire up to blast the rocket higher.

Second stage separation

Soyuz sepa

First stage separation

Soyuz rocket

The International Space Station (ISS) orbits about 400 km above Earth...

ISS

... this altitude is the same as 4,374 football pitches laid end-to-end.

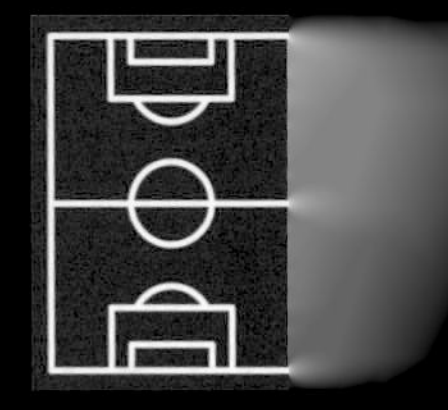

Q: What's the best way to get to the ISS and out into space?

A: On a spacecraft, such as the Russian Soyuz capsule.

During launch, an astronaut's heart rate can reach 180 beats pe minute (bpm). A normal resting heart rate is around 70 bpm.

Space rockets blast off from Earth using huge amounts of thrust. The rockets used to launch Soyuz produce 102 tonnes of thrust, reaching almost 2,000 kph and taking just nine minutes to reach space.

Docking

Over 530 astronauts have been in space, from over 38 different countries.

Imagine you are going into space for six months and only have a 1.5 kg luggage allowance – what would you take?

Docking mechanism

Orbital modules
The crew members live here while they are in orbit. This module is about 2.5 m wide. The orbital module can connect to the ISS.

When British astronaut Tim Peake went into space for the first time in December 2015, he took five items ...

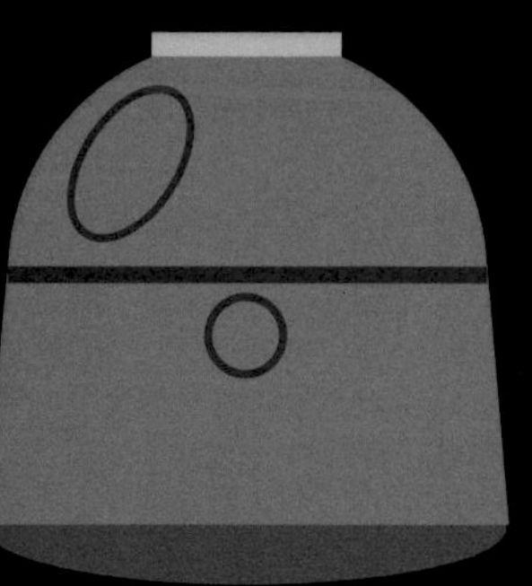

Descent module
The crew sits in this part when the Soyuz is launching to the ISS. They also use the descent module for returning to Earth.

Life support systems module
This holds things like batteries, solar panels and steering engines.

Solar panels

Astronaut

Soyuz capsule

THE INNER PLANETS

The other rocky planets are the smallest in the Solar System, but that doesn't make them less interesting. These amazing worlds have killer clouds, towering volcanoes and some of the hottest temperatures in the Solar System.

Mercury Facts
Circumference: 15,329.1 km
Distance from Sun: 0.307–0.466 AU
Time to orbit Sun: about 88 Earth days
Axis tilt: 0.034 degrees

Mercury

Messenger

Hot and cold
Mercury has no atmosphere to insulate it. On the side facing the Sun, temperatures soar to 427 °C ...

... but on the side facing away from the Sun, the temperature drops to a chilly -173 °C. Brrrrrrrr!

Mercury's *Messenger*
The *MESSENGER* probe arrived at Mercury in 2011 and orbited the planet more than 4,000 times. It made detailed map images, before it crashed into the planet's surface on 30 April 2015.

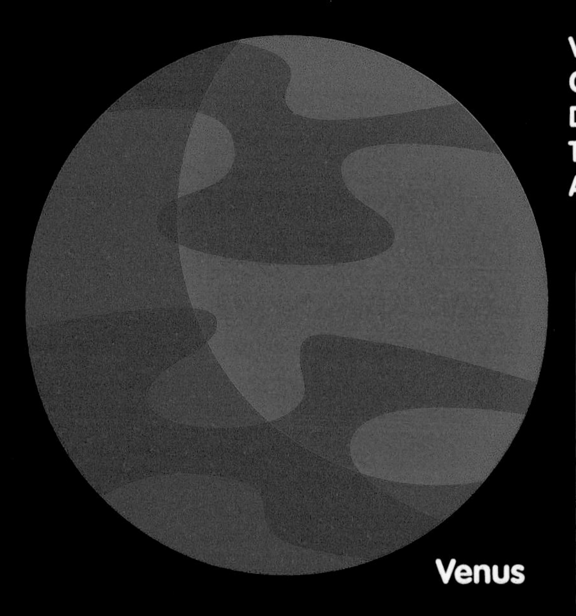
Venus

Venus Facts
Circumference: 38,024.6 km
Distance from Sun: 0.718–0.728 AU
Time to orbit Sun: about 225 Earth days
Axis tilt: 2.64 degrees

Killer planet
Venus is covered by a thick atmosphere that's nearly 97 per cent carbon dioxide. This produces a runaway greenhouse effect, pushing temperatures up to 462°C – hot enough to melt lead! The planet also has thick clouds made up of sulphuric acid droplets – not a nice place to visit!

Morning and evening star
Venus is visible as one of the brightest objects in the evening and morning sky, giving it the nicknames of the 'Morning Star' and the 'Evening Star'.

Cough! Cough!

Mars Facts
Circumference: 21,296.9 km
Distance from Sun: 1.3814–1.666 AU
Time to orbit Sun: about 687 Earth days
Axis tilt: 25.19 degrees

Q: Where would you find the biggest volcano in the Solar System?

A: Olympus Mons on Mars is about 25 km tall – that's about two and a half times the height of Mount Everest. It covers about 300,000 square km, which is about the same area as Italy.

Mars

Phobos

Lumpy moons
Mars has two small, odd-shaped moons, called Phobos and Deimos. Phobos is 27 km long and 18 km wide, while Deimos is 15 km long and 11 km wide. Their tiny size and odd shape leads many astronomers to believe that they are asteroids that have been captured by Mars's gravity.

Deimos

THE OUTER PLANETS

The outer planets are all giants. They have a small core made from metals with thick layers surrounding this made up of gases, such as hydrogen and helium, or ices, such as water, ammonia and methane.

Jupiter Facts
Circumference: 439,263.8 km
Distance from Sun: 4.9501–5.4588 AU
Time to orbit Sun: about 4,333 Earth days
Axis tilt: 3.13 degrees

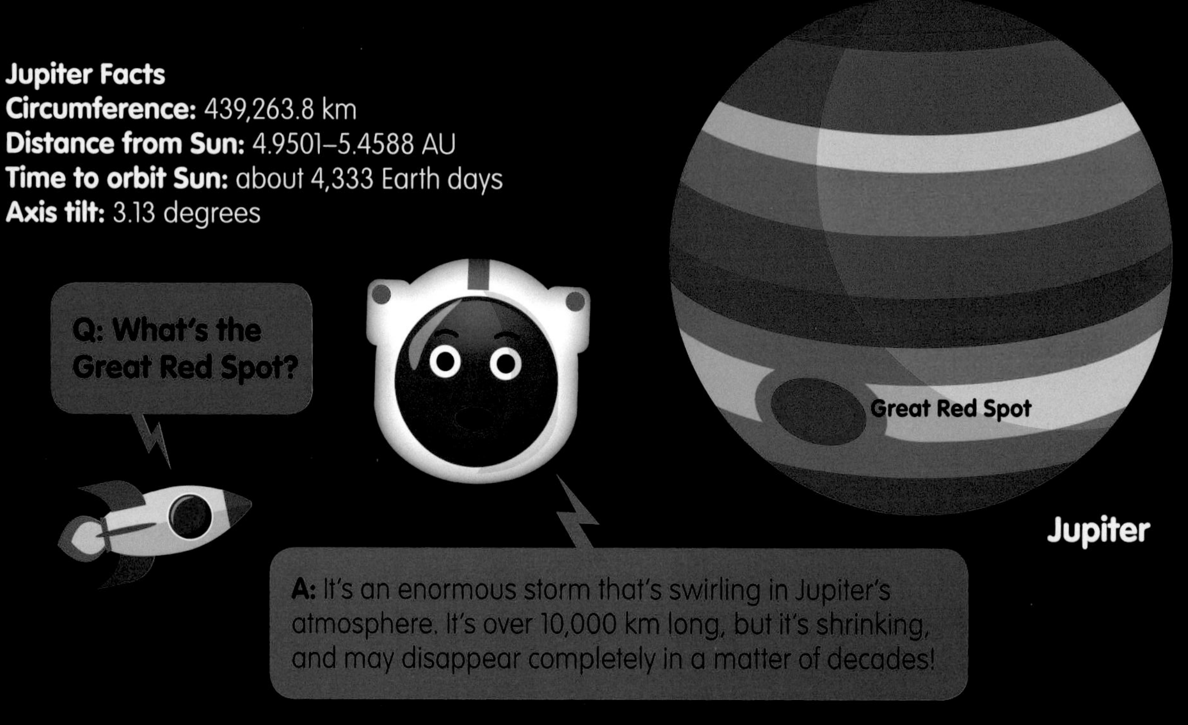

Saturn Facts
Circumference: 365,882.4 km
Distance from Sun: 9.0412–10.1238 AU
Time to orbit Sun: about 10,759 Earth days
Axis tilt: 26.73 degrees

While all of the outer planets have rings, Saturn's are the most impressive. They stretch from an altitude of 7,000 km to 80,000 km, making them 73,000 km wide, but less than 1 km thick.

The rings are made of particles that are 1 cm to 10 m in size.

Saturn

Uranus Facts
Circumference: 159,354.1 km
Distance from Sun 18.33–20.11 AU
Time to orbit Sun: about 30,689 Earth days
Axis tilt: 97.77 degrees

Uranus

Taking it easy
Uranus is actually lying down! Compared to the other planets, it's spinning around on its side. Astronomers think it was hit by a huge object early in its lifetime, knocking it over.

Neptune Facts
Circumference: 154,704.6 km
Distance from Sun 29.81–30.33 AU
Time to orbit Sun: about 60,182 Earth days
Axis tilt: 28.32 degrees

I've got terrible wind!

Q: Where would you find the strongest winds in the Solar System?

Neptune

A: Neptune's winds blow at up to 2,100 kph. It's also one of the coldest places, with cloud-top temperatures reaching just -218°C – definitely not the place for a summer holiday.

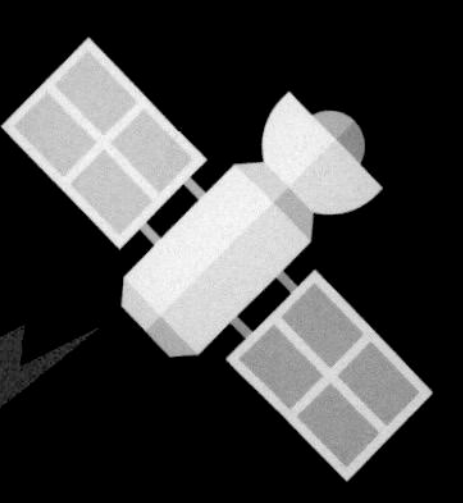

MOON ROLL CALL
Jupiter
69 known moons
Saturn
62 known and named moons with hundreds of moonlets
Uranus
27 known moons
Neptune
14 known moons

MINOR PLANETS, ASTEROIDS AND COMETS

Planets aren't the only objects orbiting the Sun. There are millions of asteroids, and countless numbers of small, minor planets and icy comets.

Q: When is a planet not a planet?

A: When it's Pluto! Until 2006, Pluto was called a planet, but the discovery of other, larger objects far out in the Solar System led to a reclassifying of the body and it was downgraded to a dwarf planet.

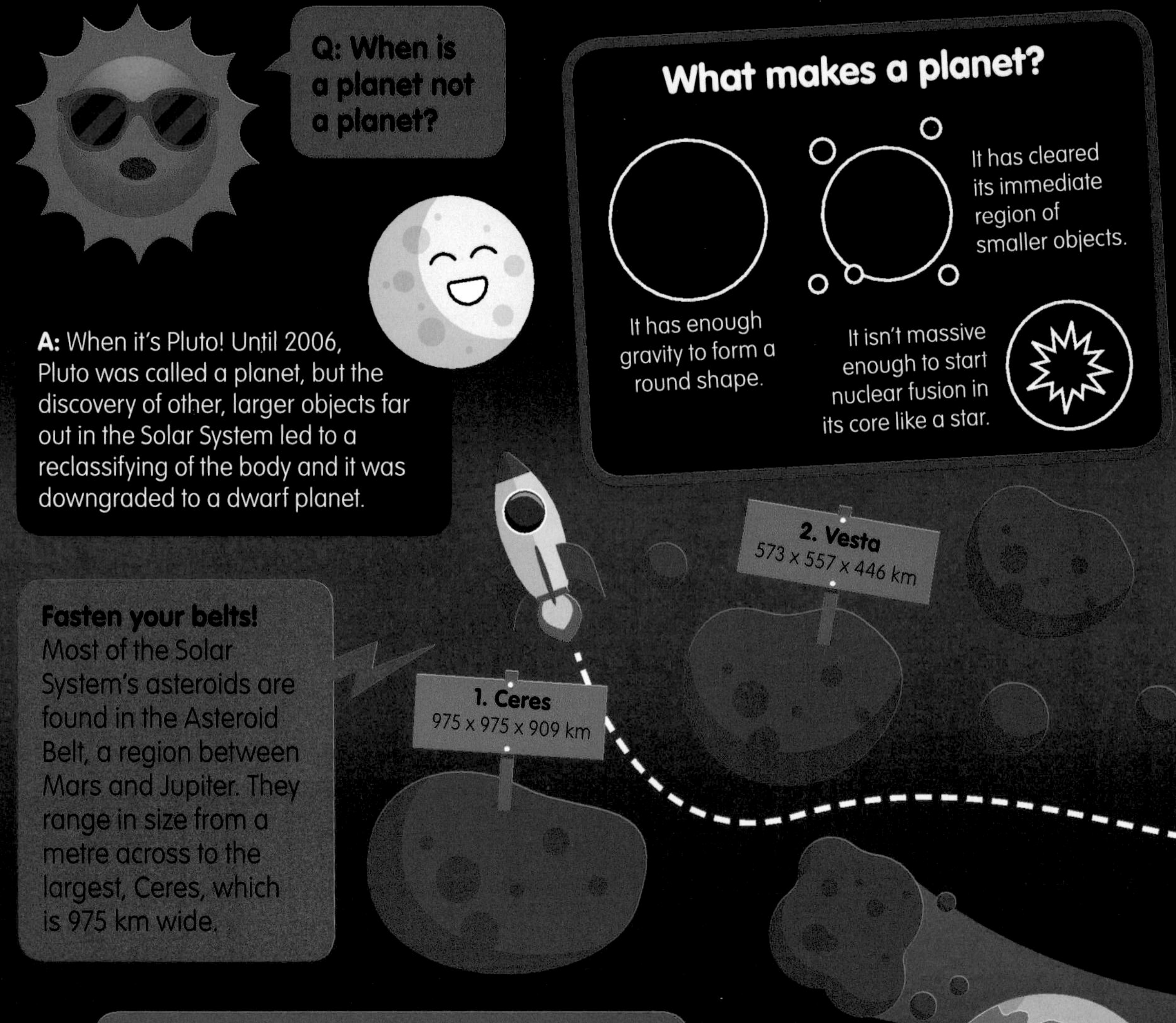

Fasten your belts!
Most of the Solar System's asteroids are found in the Asteroid Belt, a region between Mars and Jupiter. They range in size from a metre across to the largest, Ceres, which is 975 km wide.

Near miss
Some asteroids pass so close to us that they are called Near Earth Objects – and some of these actually cross Earth's orbit! As of 2016, there were nearly 14,500 of these and nearly 1,000 of them are bigger than 1 km across.

Frequent visitors?

Comets are icy visitors that produce long glowing tails as they approach the Sun. They travel in long elliptical orbits that mean they can approach the Sun every few years or only once every 100,000 years!

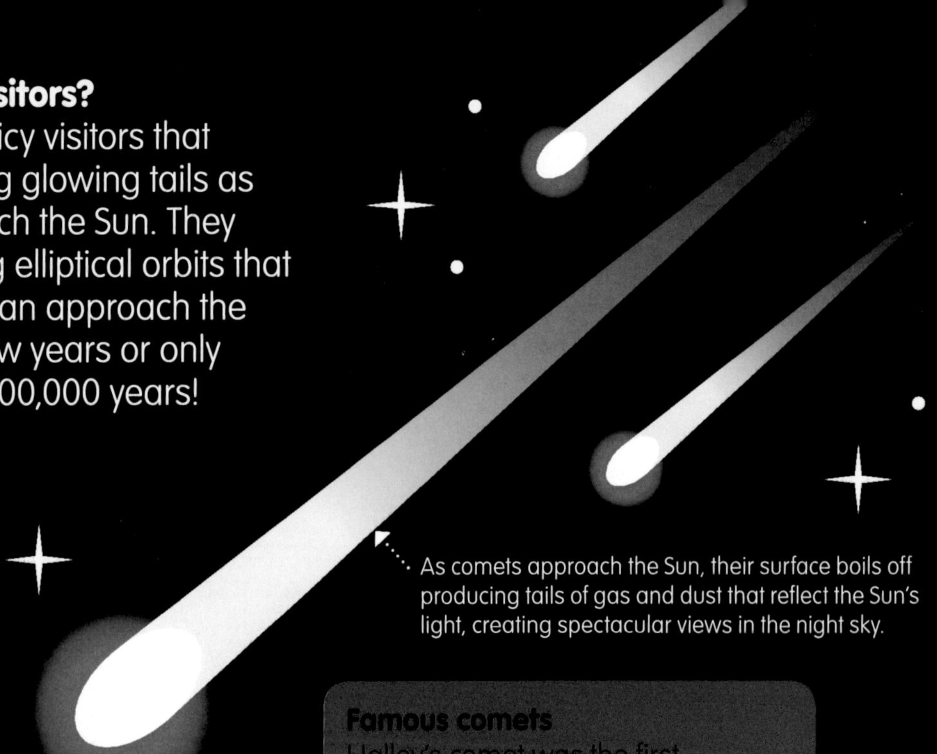

As comets approach the Sun, their surface boils off producing tails of gas and dust that reflect the Sun's light, creating spectacular views in the night sky.

Famous comets

Halley's comet was the first comet whose reappearance was accurately predicted. In 1705, English astronomer Edmund Halley (1656–1742) proved that the same comet had appeared in 1682, and also in 1607 and 1531. In fact, appearances of this comet were recorded as far back as 240 BCE. In honour of this, the comet was named after the astronomer.

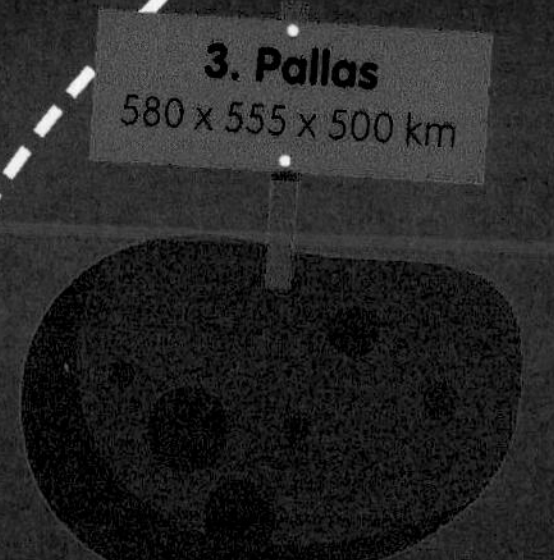

3. Pallas
580 x 555 x 500 km

4. Hygiea
530 x 407 x 370 km

EDMUND HALLEY

Comet Shoemaker-Levy 9 became famous when pieces of it slammed into Jupiter at speeds of up to 216,000 kph in July 1994. The largest impact released the same energy as 6 million megatons of TNT – about 600 times more powerful than all the world's nuclear weapons – and left a dark hole in Jupiter's atmosphere that was more than 12,000 km across! Ouch!

TYPES OF STAR

The Sun is one of trillions of stars – and it's quite a small, uninteresting one. The other stars in the Universe come in a whole range of colours and sizes, from tiny white dwarves to enormous red supergiants.

Astronomers classify the majority of stars according to their colour, temperature, size and mass. There are seven types, each with a letter, from O for the hottest to M for the coolest.

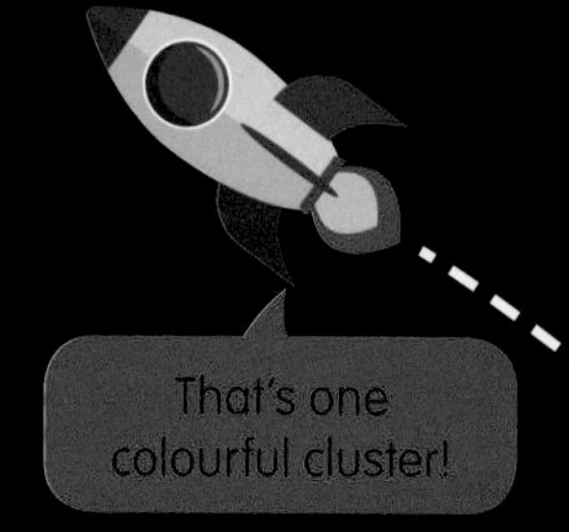

Type: O
Temperature: >30,000 K
Colour: Blue

Type: B
Temperature: 10,000–30,000 K
Colour: Blue-white

Type: A
Temperature: 7,500–10,000 K
Colour: White

Type: F
Temperature: 6,000–7,500 K
Colour: Yellow-white

Type: G
Temperature: 5,200–6,000 K
Colour: Yellow

Type: K
Temperature: 3,700–5,200 K
Colour: Light orange

Type: M
Temperature: 2,400–3,700 K
Colour: Orange-red

This system is used to classify stars during most of their lives. Just before they die, strange things happen and some stars can get VERY big (see pages 20–21).

Sun (Type G)

UY Scuti (Type M)

NML Cygni (Type M)

VY Canis Majoris (Type M)

Star giants
These are the giants of the Universe and are thousands of times bigger than our Sun. UY Scuti has a radius that is more than 1,700 times bigger than the Sun, and a volume that's 5 billion times greater. NML Cygni has a radius that is between 1,642 and 2,775 times that of the Sun. The wide range is because so much of the star is hidden by a cloud of dust. VY Canis Majoris is between 1,420 and 1,540 times bigger than the Sun.

Patterns in the sky
The night sky is divided up into different patterns of stars, called constellations. These constellations are named after mythical figures, animals and even scientific instruments.

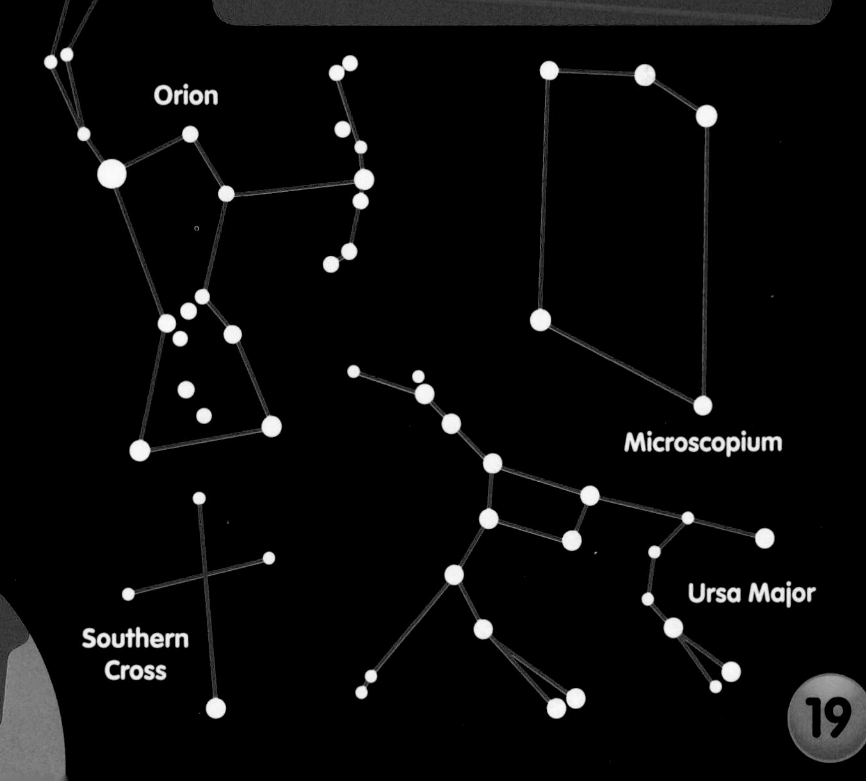

THE LIFE OF STARS

Stars don't live for ever – they are born, they shine and they die. And while some will simply fade away over billions of years, others will end their lives spectacularly in some of the most violent events in the Universe.

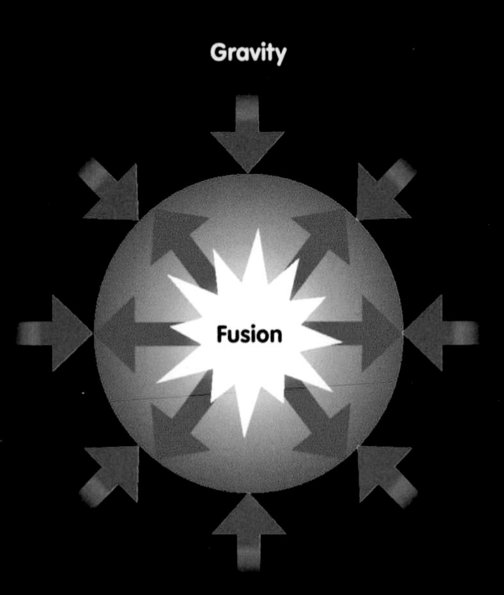

Balancing act
Stars exist through a delicate balancing act between their own force of gravity trying to crush them and the energy released by their nuclear fusion trying to blow them apart.

Life and death
How long a star lives depends on its mass. Stars are born in large clouds of gas and dust called nebulae. Clumps of gas and dust form and get bigger until they have enough gravity to start nuclear fusion and begin to shine.

Nebula

Average star

Stars that have a similar mass to our Sun will shine steadily for billions of years until they've run out of fuel.

Red giant

They'll then swell to form red giant stars before throwing off their outer layers to create round planetary nebulae, leaving a white dwarf behind.

Massive star

Stars that are more massive than the Sun will swell up at the ends of their lives to form enormous red supergiant stars.

Red supergiant

Q: How long have we got left?

A: Don't worry! Our Sun was born about 4.6 billion years ago and will continue to shine for another 4.5–5.5 billion years, so there's plenty of time left.

Q: What will happen then?

A: In about 5.4 billion years' time, the Sun will have run out of fuel. Its core will collapse under its own gravity and the Sun will grow in size, gobbling up Mercury, Venus, and maybe even Earth! It will then shrink back to form a tiny white dwarf and slowly fade away.

White dwarf

Planetary nebula

Eventually, supergiants will explode with tremendous force to produce blinding supernovae. This will leave behind small, super-dense neutron stars.

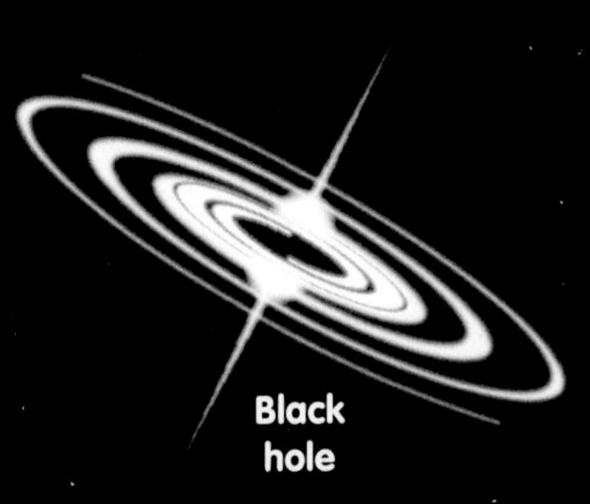

Black hole

If the stars were really massive, then they will leave behind mysterious black holes whose gravity is so strong that nothing can escape them, not even light!

Neutron star

Supernova

NEBULAE

The space between stars is far from empty. It contains gas and dust atoms that sometimes join together to form huge clouds, called nebulae.

Early astronomers believed that all smudges in the night sky were nebulae, until the work of American astronomer Edwin Hubble (1889–1953), showed that some of them were, in fact, huge galaxies of stars.

Types of nebula

Emission nebulae – these are very hot clouds of gas that glow with the energy from a nearby star.

Reflection nebulae – these clouds reflect the light of nearby stars.

Dark nebulae – these clouds block the light from stars behind them.

Planetary nebulae – these are the rings of gas and dust that are thrown off by a dying star.

Planetary nebulae get their name because they looked like planets when early astronomers viewed them through the first telescopes.

The Horsehead Nebula is a famous dark nebula that is shaped ... you guessed it ... like a horse's head! Whoa!!!!

Nebulae may look like thick clouds, but they are much less dense than any vacuum we could create here on Earth. In fact, a typical nebula the size of Earth would have a mass of just a few kilogrammes.

French astronomer Charles Messier (1730–1817), made a catalogue of 110 nebulae and star clusters so that people wouldn't mistake them for comets. Each was given a 'Messier (M) number' and these are still used today. However, some of the Messier objects are actually galaxies.

Who's gonna change our nappies?!

Star nurseries
Some nebulae are huge star factories, where clumps of gas join together and grow to form new stars and planets.

THE MILKY WAY

Stars join together to form huge galaxies, and the Milky Way is our galaxy. This enormous star city contains hundreds of billions of stars, huge clouds of gas and dust, and something very dangerous at its heart!

Q: Why is our galaxy called the Milky Way?

A: Because it forms a milky band across the night sky.

What shape is the Milky Way?
While we see the Milky Way as a milky band of stars, it is actually a barred spiral galaxy (see page 26). The band is our view of this enormous spiral, seen edge-on.

Galactic distances
Space is pretty big, and using normal everyday units, such as metres and kilometres, won't work – they're just too small. It's nearly 150 million km from Earth to the Sun. For the huge distances between stars and galaxies, astronomers use light years. This is the distance that light travels in a year and is equal to 9.5 trillion km.

Milky Way Facts

Size: 100,000-180,000 light years across, 1,000 light years thick

Number of stars: up to 400 billion

Age: 13.6 billion years

You are here

Merry go round

The Solar System is orbiting around the centre of the Milky Way at nearly 830,000 kph, but it will still take about 230 million years to complete one circuit.

Soft centre?

At the middle of the Milky Way is a huge black hole. This black hole has a mass many billions of times greater than our own Sun.

Where are we?

The Solar System lies about 30,000 light years from the centre of the Milky Way.

Are we alone?

Our galaxy is part of a group of galaxies called the Local Group. In fact, it has grown in size by gobbling up parts of this group. It will even merge with our nearest major galactic neighbour, the Andromeda Galaxy, in about 5 billion years' time.

TYPES OF GALAXY

Galaxies come in lots of different shapes – spiral, barred spiral, elliptical and irregular. They also come in many sizes, from dwarf galaxies with just a few billion stars to giants that contain up to 100 trillion!

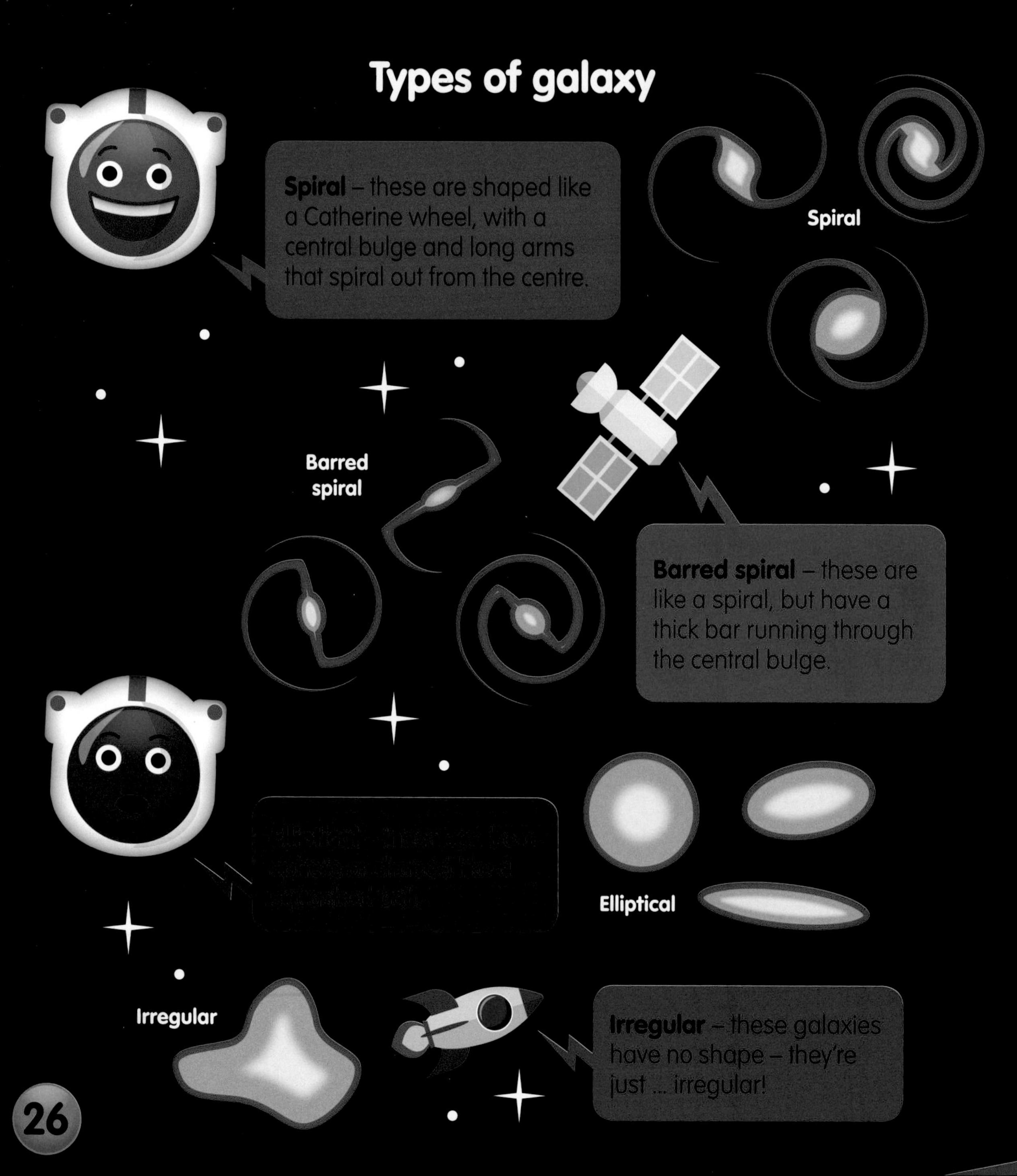

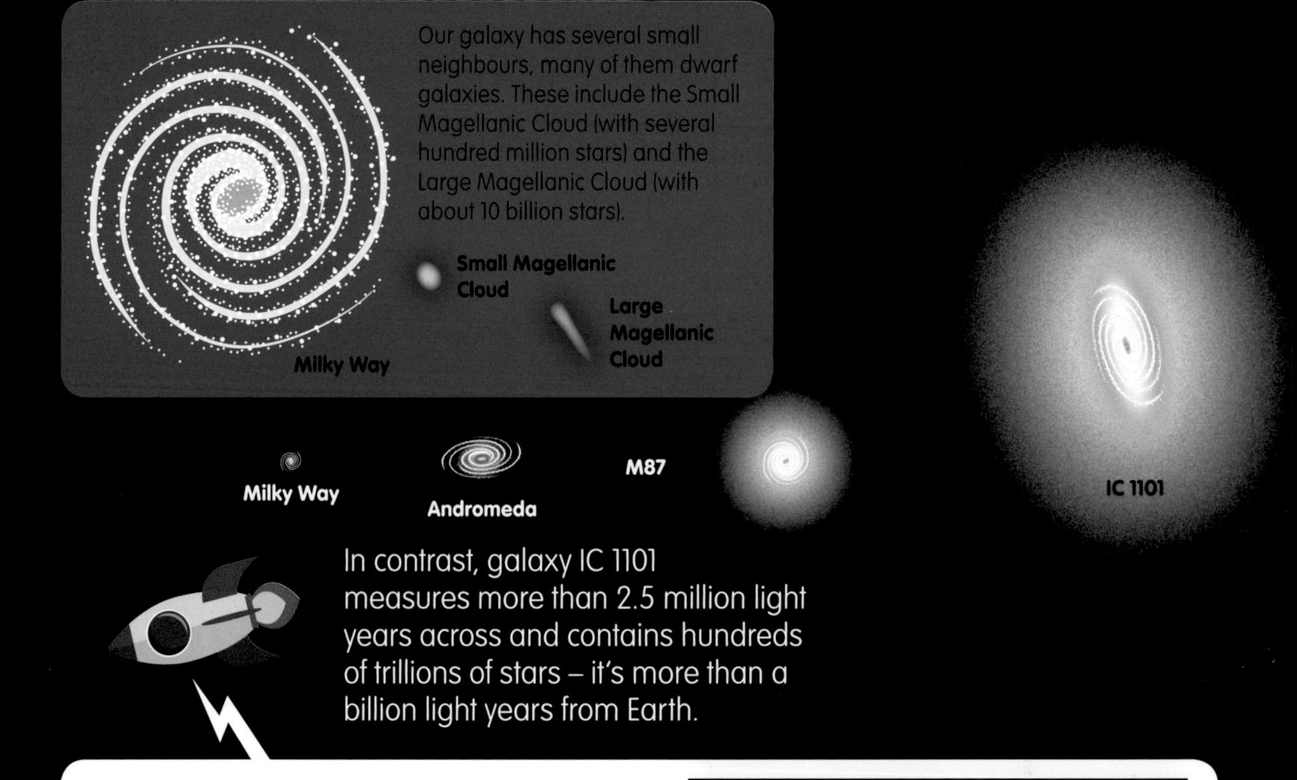

In contrast, galaxy IC 1101 measures more than 2.5 million light years across and contains hundreds of trillions of stars – it's more than a billion light years from Earth.

Galaxies are collected together in groups, which are collected in clusters, which are collected in massive superclusters. Our Milky Way is part of the Local Group, which contains 54 galaxies. 'Nearby' (well, about 54 million light years away) is the Virgo Cluster, which is made up of up to 2,000 galaxies.

Together, the Local Group and Virgo Cluster, and a few other clusters, are part of the Virgo Supercluster, a massive collection of 100 galaxy groups stretching across 110 million light years of space. And if your brain isn't blown away already, astronomers calculate that there are at least 10 million superclusters in the observable Universe!

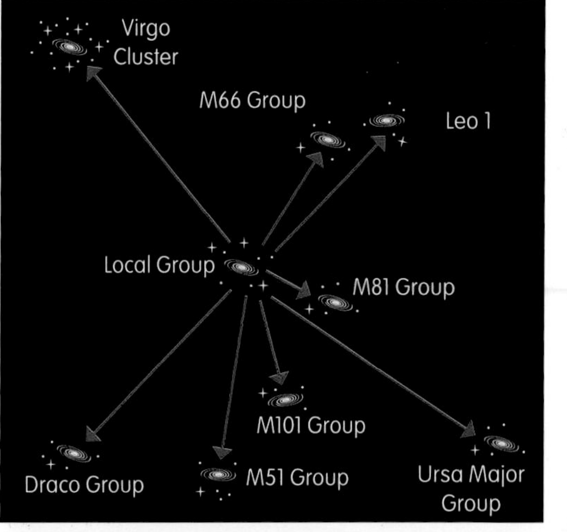

When astronomers look into space, they're looking back in time, because light from the distant Universe can take billions of years to reach us. Using powerful telescopes, such as the Hubble Space Telescope and the Keck Observatory, scientists have been able to observe galaxies that are more than 13 billion light years away!

THE BIG BANG AND WEIRD STUFF

The Universe started about 13.8 billion years ago with a bang ... a BIG bang ... a VERY big bang. And out of this amazing explosion came all the stars and galaxies that we can see, and a whole load more strange stuff that we can't even understand!

The first person to propose the theory of the Big Bang was French priest and astronomer Georges Lemaître (1894–1966). He proposed that the Universe was expanding and that it may have originated from a single point. He called his theory the 'Cosmic Egg'.

GEORGES LEMAÎTRE

Big Bang timeline

A lot happened in the first **fractions of a second.**

The fundamental forces came into existence.

The earliest elementary particles were formed.

The Universe expanded rapidly – very rapidly!

By the time the Universe was **a second** old, it had cooled to a trillion degrees.

Between three and 20 minutes after the Big Bang, the Universe had cooled to a balmy billion degrees and the earliest atomic nuclei formed.

Up to 240,000 years after the Big Bang, the Universe was made up of a hot, opaque soup of atomic nuclei and electrons.

Some 200–600 million years after the Big Bang, the first stars and galaxies formed.

Up to 150 million years after the Big Bang, the Universe cooled and became transparent and went dark, before any stars formed.

About
years
Big Ba
Sun an
System

Scared of the dark?
While we can see plenty of stuff in the night sky, astronomers believe that there is a lot more out there that we cannot see. Some of this is holding galaxies together and astronomers call this dark matter. However, something else is pushing the galaxies apart, and astronomers call this stuff dark energy – they just don't know what these mysterious forces are!

GLOSSARY

ASTEROID
A small, rocky body, or minor planet, that orbits the Sun.

ATMOSPHERE
The layer of mixed gases that surrounds Earth, as well as other planets.

ATOMIC NUCLEUS
The small, dense centre of an atom, made up of protons and neutrons that are tightly bound together.

AXIS
An imaginary line that passes straight through the centre of a planet. A planet rotates around its axis.

CIRCUMFERENCE
The total distance around the edge of a circle, or any other complete, curved shape.

CONSTELLATION
A recognisable group of stars that form a pattern, often named after an animal or mythological character.

CONVECTIVE ZONE
Found between a star's core and outer surface, this is where heat rises towards the surface, cools, and falls towards the core to be heated again, transferring energy.

CORE
The innermost point of a planet or star. In stars, this is where energy is released in the form of nuclear fusion.

ECOSYSTEM
All the living things within a given environment, including plants, animals and smaller organisms, and how they interact with each other.

ELLIPTICAL
Oval-shaped, like a squashed circle. Many comets have elliptical orbits around the Sun.

GPS
An abbreviation of Global Positioning System. GPS is a satellite-based navigation system that can show the location of a person or thing.

KELVIN
Kelvin (K) is a measure of temperature where zero K is equal to -273°C – the coldest temperature possible (absolute zero).

MASS
The amount of matter within an object, regardless of its weight or volume. An object with a higher density will also have more mass.

NEUTRON STAR
The collapsed core of a large star. This is the smallest and densest type of star, composed mainly of tightly packed neutrons.

NUCLEAR FUSION
When two atomic nuclei join together to form a large nucleus, releasing energy.

NUCLEAR WEAPON
A powerful explosive device that releases huge amounts of energy, created by nuclear reactions.

ORBIT
A regular, repeating path of an object in space around another object, for example a moon, planet or star.

RADIATION
Energy that is transmitted or radiated in the form of waves or particles, including radio waves, microwaves and visible light.

RADIATIVE ZONE
The inner layer of a star, closest to the core, where energy from the star's super-hot core radiates outwards.

RADIUS
The distance between the centre of a circle and its circumference, measured in a straight line.

RED SUPERGIANT
When a star runs out of hydrogen, needed for nuclear fusion, it swells to become a red giant or supergiant – the largest star in the known universe.

SATELLITE
Any object in space that orbits a planet or star. It can be natural, like a moon, or man-made, like the International Space Station in Earth's orbit.

SOLAR PANEL
A device that absorbs energy from the Sun and converts it into usable electrical power.

SULPHURIC ACID
A very strong acid with the chemical formula H_2SO_4.

THRUST
A force that pushes an object or a vehicle along in a particular direction.

TNT
Short for trinitrotoluene, this is a very powerful explosive material.

VACUUM
A region that contains no air or other gases.

VOLUME
The amount of three-dimensional space that an object holds or occupies.

WHITE DWARF
A type of very small star that usually marks the last stage of a star's life.

INDEX